Wild Weather

Flood

REVISED AND UPDATED

Catherine Chambers

www.heinemann.co.uk/library

Visit our website to find out more information about **Heinemann Library** books.

To order:

☎ Phone ++44 (0)1865 888112

🖺 Send a fax to ++44 (0)1865 314091

🖥 Visit the Heinemann Bookshop at www.heinemann.co.uk/library to browse our catalogue and order online.

First published in Great Britain by Heinemann Library, Halley Court, Jordan Hill, Oxford OX2 8EJ, part of Harcourt Education. Heinemann is a registered trademark of Harcourt Education.

Editorial: Clare Lewis
Designed: Steve Mead and Q2A
Illustrations: Paul Bale
Picture Research: Tracy Cummins
Production: Julie Carter

Originated by Modern Age Repro
Printed and bound in China by South China Printing Company Limited

10 digit ISBN 0 431 15080 X
13 digit ISBN 978 0 431 15080 2

11 10 09 08 07
10 9 8 7 6 5 4 3 2 1

British Library Cataloguing in Publication Data

Chambers, Catherine
Wild Weather: Flood. – 2nd Edition – Juvenile literature
551.4'89
A full catalogue record for this book is available from the British Library.

Acknowledgements
The Publishers would like to thank the following for permission to reproduce photographs: Aerial Archives/Alamy p14, AP Photo/Vincent Laforet, POOL p15, Ardea p5, Corbis pp16, 17, 23, 24, James Davis, Eye Ubiquitous/Corbis p29, Ecoscene pp4, 8, 10, 12, 25, EPA (PA photos) p22, Getty Images/PhotoDisc p28, Oxford Scientific Films pp9, 11, 19, PA Photos pp21, 27, Reuters p18, Reuters/Miro Kuzmanovic MIK p13, Rex Features p26, Robert Harding Picture Library p20, Still Pictures p7.

Cover photograph of floods in New Orleans, USA, reproduced with permission of Radhika Chalasani/Getty Images.

The Publishers would like to thank Mark Rogers and the Met Office for their assistance with the preparation of this book.

Every effort has been made to contact copyright holders of any material reproduced in this book.
Any omissions will be rectified in subsequent printings if notice is given to the Publisher.

The paper used to print this book comes from sustainable resources.

Any words appearing in the text in bold, **like this**, are explained in the Glossary.

Contents

What is a flood?

A flood is when water covers the land. Heavy rain makes river waters spill over their **banks**. Storms can make huge sea waves that flood the coast.

■ *These houses are on **stilts**. They are safe from the flood waters.*

■ *The water flooded roads and buildings.*

This is North Dakota in the United States. In April 2006, the waters of the great Red River burst its banks. People were forced to leave their homes.

Where do floods happen?

Floods happen mostly where there are lots of storms. Storms bring heavy rain and strong winds. This can cause rivers to flood.

■ *The areas in blue are places where floods often happen.*

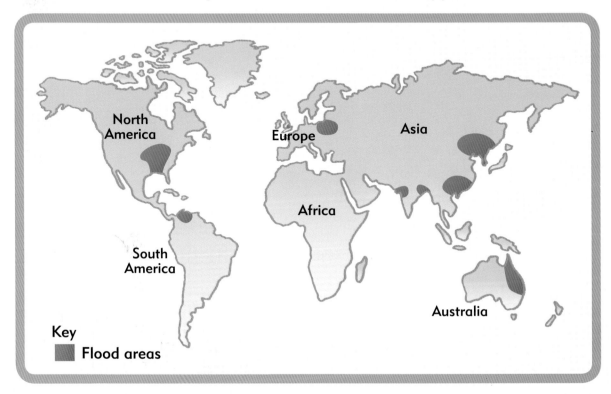

North America

Europe

Asia

Africa

South America

Australia

Key

Flood areas

■ *Floods often happen in Bangladesh.*

This flood is in the country of Bangladesh. Bangladesh gets a lot of heavy rain from June to September. This time is called the wet monsoon season.

Where does rain come from?

Winds blow over the sea. They pick up tiny drops of **water vapour**. As air rises into the sky it cools and the water vapour turns into small droplets of water. These droplets make clouds.

■ *Clouds form above the sea.*

■ *Rain falls from large dark clouds.*

If the droplets join together they become too heavy and fall to the ground as rain. If there is too much rain in one place it can cause floods.

Why do floods happen?

This is a river **flood plain**. When heavy rain falls the river can become too full. The water rises above the **banks** and spills on to the flood plain.

■ *These fields are sometimes flooded by the river.*

■ *This coast is in danger of being flooded.*

Strong winds blow across the sea during storms.
This makes the water into huge waves. These
rise over the shore and cause floods along
the coast.

W at are floo s like?

Sometimes floodwaters rise slowly. People have time to get ready for the flood. At other times floodwaters rise quickly. People and cars get caught in the flood.

■ *This river is full and ready to burst its banks.*

The water makes anything inside buildings get wet. Some things are washed away. The water also brings a lot of dirt. This dirt has been picked up by the floodwaters.

New Orleans floo

This is New Orleans in the United States. The city lies on low land near the coast. **Flood defences** have been built to try and stop the city from flooding.

■ *The city of New Orleans is always at risk of flooding.*

■ *Buildings in New Orleans were badly flooded in 2005.*

In 2005, a large storm called a hurricane made some huge waves. These waves broke the flood defences and the city was flooded. People had to leave their homes.

Harmful floods

Floodwaters trap people and animals. Roads and bridges are flooded and broken. It can be harder to find fresh food or clean drinking water.

■ *Animals can be trapped by floodwaters.*

■ *The flood has left debris in the town.*

Huge waves have flooded this coast. Boats and buildings are damaged. Roads are covered in sand and stones. Fish, seabirds, and seaweed are washed up onto the shore.

elpful floods

In Bangladesh, plants rot in the floodwaters. The rotted plants in the water help to make **fertile** soil. Rice **crops** grow well in this soil.

■ *Floods can be good to soil and crops in Bangladesh.*

A river flows very fast when there is a lot of rain. The fast river washes down a lot of mud. The mud settles on flooded fields. This can make the soil in these fields more fertile.

■ *This river is picking up mud as it flows.*

Preparing for floods

Weather stations ask radio and television stations to warn people about floods. The most serious warning is the **flood alert**.

■ *A flood alert warns people to get ready for floods.*

■ *These men are stacking sandbags along a river in case it floods.*

People move their furniture upstairs. They switch off the electricity. Sandbags are stacked against doors and along rivers. This stops water from reaching houses. Some people leave their homes.

Coping with floods

In some countries there are bad floods nearly every year. So **flood shelters** are built on high ground. People hurry to these shelters when there is a flood.

■ *Sometimes it is safer to stay in a shelter during a flood.*

■ *People have to travel by boat if roads are flooded.*

Floodwaters can cover roads for many days. The water stops car and bus engines from working. So people can only travel around by boat or by air.

Living with floods

This is an area that often floods. So people have built **platforms** on **stilts**. Cows, chickens, and other farm animals are kept safe until the floodwaters go down.

■ *These animals are safe from the flood.*

■ *Too much water can be bad for rice crops.*

Rice is a **crop** that grows in flooded fields, but heavy flooding destroys rice and other crops. They are battered by the flowing water. Then they rot in the ground.

To the rescue!

The country of Mozambique was badly flooded in 2000. Helicopters rescued people from trees and high ground. They dropped food and equipment to make clean drinking water.

■ *People were rescued from trees by helicopters.*

■ *Boats can be used to rescue people.*

Sea **lifeboats** are being used to rescue these people from their flooded homes. The rescuers are taking the people to places that are above the flood. There they will find food and warmth.

More floods?

The Earth's climate is changing all the time. At the moment it seems to be getting warmer. This is called "global warming". Some scientists think that this will bring more floods.

■ *The white patches over Earth are clouds.*

■ *Warm weather causes snow and ice to melt.*

Scientists believe global warming will cause some of the ice in arctic regions to melt. This will raise the sea level and cause more floods in coastal areas.

More books to read

Nature's Patterns: *The Water Cycle*, Monica Hughes (Heinemann Library, 2005).

The Weather: *Rain*, Angela Royston (Chrysalis Children's Books, 2004)

Index

Titles in the *Wild Weather* series include:

Hardback 978-0-431-15081-9

Hardback 978-0-431-15082-6

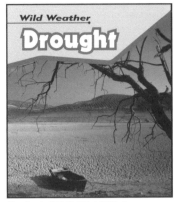

Hardback 978-0-431-15083-3

Hardback 978-0-431-15080-2

Hardback 978-0-431-15085-7

Hardback 978-0-431-15086-4

Hardback 978-0-431-15087-1

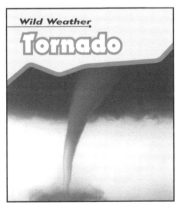

Hardback 978-0-431-15088-8

Find out about other titles Heinemann Library on our website www.heinemann.co.uk/library